Highest, Longest, Deepest

Contents

Written by Jilly Hunt

Collins

Humans enjoy exploring the highest, longest or deepest things around them.

Some of us dream of constructing the highest, longest or deepest thing. Computers help with planning how to do it.

Highest

High up in the clouds is Mount Everest. It is the highest peak at about 8848 m high.

The highest tower block reaches for the skies. It is 828 m from the ground.

It has the highest lookout point at about 556 m.

The first ever tower block was just 42 m high!

Blue sea swirls round this mound of rock.
It is the highest **sea stack** at 561 m high.

Sea birds rest on its steep peak.

This is the highest statue at 182 m.

You can see a long way from the statue's lookout point at 135 m.

Longest

There is an argument about the longest river!
Rivers in Africa and South America are each
a similar length. The river in Africa is considered
to be 6695 km long.

The river in South America is considered to be 6750 km long.

Rivers can cut away firm ground to form
a steep **canyon**.

The longest canyon is the deepest one too!
It is about 5300 m deep and 500,000 m long.

The longest high-speed railway is 2298 km.
This train travels at 320 kmph.
The longest railway trip on one train is 10,214 km.

The biggest **avenue** is 110 m across.
It's a long way across.

Deepest

The deepest point of the sea is a **trench** that lies about 10,994 m down. The trench is deeper than Mount Everest is high.

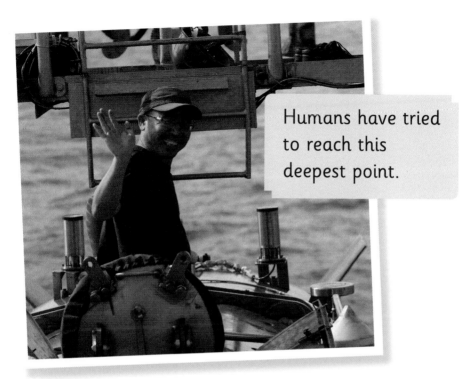

Humans have tried to reach this deepest point.

The deepest pool is the biggest too. It is around 1600 m deep.

About 330 streams and rivers lead into it.

The deepest swimming pool is 60.02 m deep.
Fearless swimmers train here.

avenue street, way

canyon long, deep land cut by a river

sea stack mound of rock in the sea

trench long ditch on land or under the sea

Index

Highest

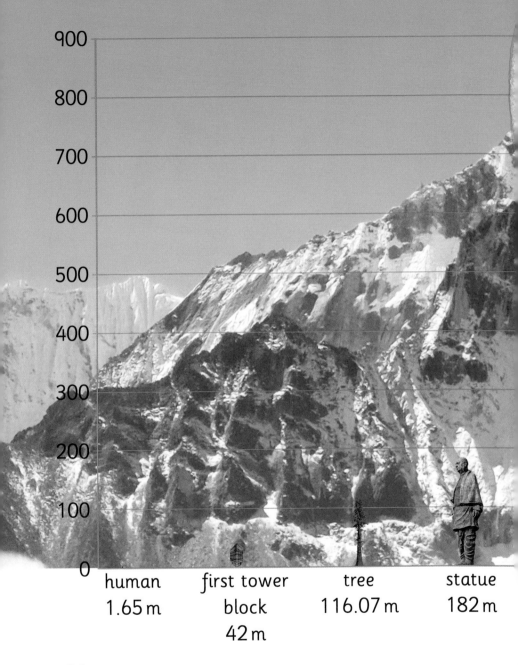

900	
800	
700	
600	
500	
400	
300	
200	
100	
0	

human
1.65 m

first tower
block
42 m

tree
116.07 m

statue
182 m

sea stack
561 m

tower block
828 m

Mount Everest
8848 m

Map

longest river in South America

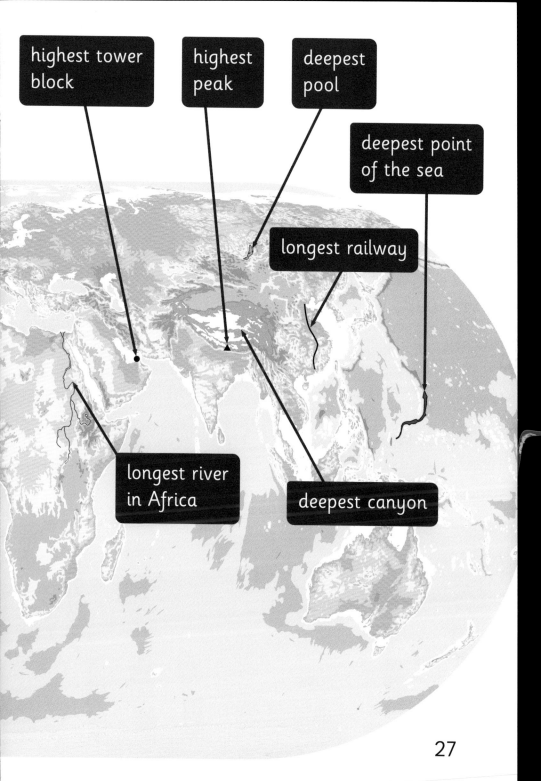

highest tower block

highest peak

deepest pool

deepest point of the sea

longest railway

longest river in Africa

deepest canyon

Tower facts

Read some fantastic facts about the highest tower.
It has:

39,000,000 kg of steel

the longest lift

the lift travels at
10 m per second

at least 4 swimming pools

the highest swimming pool
at about 270 m

Highest, longest, deepest

🐾 Review: After reading 🐾

Use your assessment from hearing the children read to choose any GPCs, words or tricky words that need additional practice.

Read 1: Decoding

- Challenge the children to find the words in bold and work out their meaning in the sentence where they appear:
  page 8: **sea stack** page 14: **canyon** page 17: **avenue**
  o Ask the children to check they were right by reading the definitions in the glossary on page 22.
- Challenge the children to identify the /oo/ or /yoo/ sound in these words:
  avenue (/**yoo**/) blue (/**oo**/) statue (/**yoo**/)
  humans (/**yoo**/) argument (/**yoo**/)
- Turn to pages 8 and 9. Point to: **sea**, **swirls**, **birds**, **peak**. Say: Can you blend in your head when you read these words?

Read 2: Prosody

- Model reading page 6, emphasising **highest** and **828 m**. Discuss the effect of emphasising important facts.
- Challenge the children to read page 7 to themselves first, and to choose which words they think are the most important to emphasise.
- Ask children to take turns to read a sentence and discuss their choice of emphasised words.
- Bonus content: Ask the children to read the word labels on pages 26 and 27 using emphasis and a variety of tones, as if they were a broadcaster who must hold their viewers' attention.

Read 3: Comprehension

- Encourage the children to talk about the highest and longest places in their local area, i.e. the highest building, the longest school corridor.
- Ask the children what is special about all the things in this book.
  (e.g. *they are record breakers, they are extreme, they are unique*) Can the children suggest an alternative book title? (e.g. *Record Breakers*)
- Ask the following to help children practise skimming and scanning skills.
  o Is this book just about things made by people? What else does it include?
- Challenge the children to find the number facts for the: deepest pool (*page 20: 1600 m*), deepest canyon (*page 15: 5300 m deep*)
- Look together at pages 30 and 31. Can children remember a fact about each picture? Encourage them to look back in the book if necessary.
- Bonus content: Using pages 24 and 25, challenge the children to describe the items on the graph, using vocabulary from the previous pages.